Uncommon Praises From Common Psalms

Vol. 1

Psalms 1 - 30

John H. Hill

Uncommon Praises from Common Psalms

Copyright 2011 © by John H. Hill

Uncommon Praises from Common Psalms, vol. 1
By John H. Hill

Printed in the United States of America

ISBN 978-1-257-09025-9

All rights reserved solely by the author. The author guarantees all contents are original and do not infringe upon the legal rights of any other person or work. No part of this book may be reproduced in any form without the written permission from the author.

Unless otherwise indicated, Bible quotations are taken from the Authorized Version (KJV) of the Bible (Public Domain) and from the author's personal translations (*a personal translation*) of the Holy Scriptures.

Cover art is from Public Domain files.

Dedication

To my church, the people of First Emmanuel Baptist Church in Summerville, SC who have been of the Berean ilk of the New Testament. Their desire for knowledge, understanding, and application of God's Word has led them to a consistent walk with our Savior.

Their desire to know Christ through His Word has made me a better student and teacher as I prepare myself and my notes for presentation.

Uncommon Praises from Common Psalms

Forward

These devotional studies were developed as our church studied the Psalms on Wednesday evenings during our weekly Bible Study and Prayer meeting. They are not intended to be an exhaustive study of each Psalm, but simple thoughts from selected verses.

Various writers offer to us emotional ups and downs as we read of their spiritual struggles in their attempts of aligning faith with circumstances. There is joy, triumph, depression, disillusionment, sadness, and a host of other feelings.

While David is the most prolific of the authors, the Psalms include others who have shared with us their lives openly for all to see.

In the end, the answer to all problems and predicaments is always found in the Rock – the Lord Jesus Christ. He is the only One sufficient to meet all our needs and heal all our heartaches.

My desire is that these devotionals might point you to the One who loves you and cares for you more than anyone else.

John H. Hill

Contents

God Knows (Psalm 1.6)	7
God's Laughter (Psalm 2.4)	9
Deliverance (Psalm 3.8)	11
What Makes You Tremble? (Psalm 4.4)	13
Lead me, O LORD (Psalm 5.8)	15
The Bass in God's Choir (Psalm 6.1)	17
How to Treat Your Enemy (Psalm 7.4)	19
Arrogance and Judgment (Psalm 8.3, 4)	21
A Matter of Perspective (Psalm 9.9)	23
Standing One's Ground (Psalm 10.6)	25
Foundations (Psalm 11.3)	27
Much Ado about Nothing (Psalm 12.2)	29
Patience (Psalm 13.1, 2)	31
The Fool (Psalm 14.1a)	33
Communion (Psalm 15.1)	35
Security Blankets (Psalm 16.5)	37
Innocent Perspective (Psalm 17.3)	39
The Rock (Psalm 18.2)	41
Sunday Mouth (Psalm 19.14)	43
Offering or Sacrifice (Psalm 20.3)	45
Career or Calling (Psalm 21.6, 7)	47
The Worm (Psalm 22.6)	49
Satisfaction and Sufficiency (Psalm 23.1, 2)	51
The King of Glory (Psalm 24.7, 8)	53
Attitudes and Actions (Psalm 25.4)	55
Integrity (Psalm 26.1, 2)	57
A One-Track Mind (Psalm 27.4)	59

Uncommon Praises from Common Psalms

Help (Psalm 28.1)   61
The Voice (Psalm 29)   63
Night (Psalm 30.5)   65

God Knows

"For the LORD knoweth the way of the righteous: but the way of the ungodly shall perish." Psalm 1.6

When my wife and I were dating, we spent some time "getting to know" one another. To some these days, that seems to be a lost art. The world propagates the idea that a couple must try physical intimacy in order to determine whether or not they are compatible for marriage.

After living together for some time, the couple goes through a learning process that sometimes isn't one that leads to the marriage altar. The problem is that they have the cart before the horse (an old saying that shows my age). Although the worldling would never admit this, a biblical approach makes much more sense. Why not wait for physical satisfaction and enjoy getting to know each other.

For young people, this may be hard to believe; but as physical beauty moves to aches, pains, and wrinkles, inner beauty becomes more pronounced with age. Ultimately, the physical succumbs to the spiritual as a couple grows in age and wisdom. A marriage based only upon physical attraction is doomed to failure (take a look at Hollywood celebrities). After 35 years of marriage, I can honestly say my wife is more attractive now than when she was 20. Over the years our lives have grown together – becoming one with each other in ways that we never dreamed of when dating.

The psalmist acknowledges this when he says, *"For the LORD* (Jehovah – "the existing One" {the covenant and saving One}) *knoweth the way of the righteous..."* In the Hebrew, the word "knoweth" is an active participle meaning that He is continually knowing the righteous. There is never a time in the believer's life when God is not addressing His attention in our direction.

If that doesn't give you cause to shout, the Hebrew word "yada," knoweth, means more than simply being acquainted with the fact that someone is out there somewhere. While it speaks of acquaintance, it is also applied to an intimate relationship. This is

Uncommon Praises from Common Psalms

one of the great blessings associated with salvation. Salvation is so much more than a fire escape from hell; it is an intimate relationship with the great God of Creation. The more you walk with God, the closer becomes the relationship.

Being in the company of God establishes the believer's way; we are never alone and never on our own. God cares. The ungodly, on their own way without divine help, can only come to destruction because their way is finite. The believer, known by God, can never eternally fail because God is with him.

God's Laughter

"He that sitteth in the heavens shall laugh: the Lord shall have them in derision." Psalm 2.4

Do you ever find yourself puzzled over questions that seem to have no answer? Maybe I'm different, but I like to know the answers to problems and I like to have facts upon which to base my conclusions.

Psalm 2 is a fitting second psalm to the Hebrew Psalter. While Psalm 1 speaks of a proper attitude as we approach God in worship, Psalm 2 speaks of the majesty of the One we worship. It shows the distinction between the worshiper and the object of worship.

Consider the vanity of humanity. It seems that everyone's world is defined by their own specialized view of their surroundings. The two-year old has a limited worldview, but they have a desire to control their sphere of influence. An adult would look at the tyke's aggressive behavior in protecting and controlling his world as either cute, a rite of passage, or maybe something to be addressed through disciplinary actions. His ability to reach beyond his sphere is limited and so the adult will often laugh – sometimes in derision at his inability to really change his environment. After all, the walls of the playpen are restrictive.

That sphere grows with age. The teenager who now has a driver's license may expand their horizons, but they are still limited by finances, age restrictions, etc. The housewife may expand her influence beyond the home, but it is still limited by her personal abilities or inabilities. The man of the house, who boasts of "being the man" is limited. He may be the king of his castle-home, but his influence and real ability to change things is limited.

There are those, however, who have stepped outside normal limitations and have become political leaders. These are really "big" people with great influence. They often have high hopes and great dreams of accomplishment. With them, things will be different.

Uncommon Praises from Common Psalms

Their motto is: "When I'm at the helm, the ship will reach a fair haven." They imagine a vain (unobtainable dream, Psalm 2.1) thing because they are quite limited when all is considered. Many have great power by comparison to the rest of humanity – the President of the United States with all of the combined members of Congress and the Supreme Court – together they wield more power than an average person can imagine. But they are limited.

When God looks down on the raging masses, whether great or small, all are nothing more than a vapor that appears for a while and vanishes away. (James 4.14) The greatest aspirations of the greatest humans ever to live are but a puff of wind when placed next to the greatness of the Almighty. The cruelest of tyrants and the proudest accomplishments coupled with human arrogance is nothing more than a drop of water in the ocean of eternity.

Consider God. Limitless. Unbounded by any walls or restrictions. As He looks down on an arrogant world which thinks it can make its own way and provide for its own safety, He sees impotence and inability. While humanity can control on that which is within its realm of influence, the Almighty God controls all. His power is unlimited and His ability to protect is unchallenged.

Don't forget – this Almighty God is vitally concerned with you and your situation. He knows you personally and cares. While your congressman may be too busy with his life, God is never overwhelmed. He is always there and available to those who trust in Him. (Psalm 2.12b)

Deliverance

"Salvation belongeth unto the LORD: thy blessing is upon thy people. Selah."
Psalm 3.8

According to the title of this Psalm, the events surrounding Psalm 3 were based in Absalom's rebellion against his father David. (See II Samuel 15) Absalom, who had been spoiled partly because of David's own feelings of personal guilt and culpability, had begun a campaign to steal the hearts of the inhabitants of Jerusalem. His plan worked well.

In the middle of the night, David fled from Jerusalem in such haste that he went barefoot up and across the Mount of Olives. In tears he fled. Surrounded by many who were close friends, family and military warriors David felt all alone.

There is nothing quite like the feeling we get when a family member, or a trusted confidant, deserts us. When someone distant leaves us, the loss is minimal; however, when your "bff" (best friend forever) walks out on you it seems to matter little who is left. There is that hit in the pit of your stomach – that nauseating feeling that lets you know there is nothing you can do to change the situation. Nothing you can do will bring that friend back.

At that time, it doesn't matter who is left – your best friend is gone.

While we neither minimize the hurt nor the loss; David came to a real discovery. "Salvation belongeth to the LORD." The word "salvation" is the same word translated "help" in verse 2. It means salvation and deliverance. In this context it does not refer to the salvation of David's eternal soul, but to his deliverance from his hurtful circumstances.

Even though it is a wonderful thing to have friends - close friends, it is a better thing to put your trust and confidence in the LORD. Friends will often disappoint. Friends, while in the immediate vicinity, can only be present during your trials. They may cry with

Uncommon Praises from Common Psalms

you; empathize with you. But God helps. God delivers. God gives sleep and rest. God gives blessing.

Remember, no matter what is your situation in life, you are not alone.

What makes you tremble?

"Stand in awe, and sin not: commune with your own heart upon your bed, and be still. Selah." Psalm 4.4

This morning my wife forwarded an e-mail to me. It was from a friend living in Florida with an attached picture of her pool. Under a patio table was a snake – about 5 feet long. The caption under the picture read: "What a way to get your juices flowing in the A.M." Although I have never made any personal friends of snakes, they have not caused me to quiver inside either.

Some things should make us quiver. In Psalm 4.4, the word "awe" means to quiver, tremble, or to shake. It is in the imperative mood meaning this is a command. By application, "to stand in awe" means to be so frightened or so angry that the body trembles uncontrollably. Within the context of Psalm 4, "to stand in awe" is associated with fear rather than anger.

So what is it that causes you to be so afraid that you lose control of your body's stability? What frightens you so much that you can do nothing but cringe in fear?

The psalmist quotes God, *"O ye sons of men, how long will ye turn my glory into shame: how long will ye love vanity, and seek after leasing {deceit}? Selah."* (Psalm 4.2) What had caused the psalmist to fear with uncontrollable terror was the prospect of misrepresenting or falling short of pleasing God. "Sin not" is similar to the Greek meaning "to fall short." It is in the imperfect mood suggesting an unfinished, continuing action. David was filled with terror when he considered the possibility of offending God.

He had little or no concern for what people said. He cared not that a popular movie star or a local politician valued his opinion. He was oblivious to whether the latest star in the music industry even noticed his existence. He had not even heard of soccer or baseball.

His only concern was – "Is God pleased with me?"

Uncommon Praises from Common Psalms

At the end of the day — at the end of your life - it matters little of your stature in society or of your wealth. What matters is your stand (relationship) with God.

Lead me, O LORD

"Lead me, O LORD, in thy righteousness because of mine enemies; make thy way straight before my face." Psalm 5.8

The story of Pinocchio is about a carved doll who became a real boy. Although his creator loved him dearly, some fast-talking deceivers (Honest John and Gideon) were able to lure him to Pleasure Island through promises of fun and excitement.

Pinocchio's downfall was that he forgot the love of Geppetto and he was inexperienced.

Flattery has led more people to destruction than can probably be numbered. It is as old as Creation itself. This was the attraction the Serpent had over Eve and it is a similar attraction still used today. When coupled with the arrogant attitude by individuals who believe they can handle their own problems, failure and slavery is certain.

Parents expect this kind of attraction for children who are inexperienced. That's one of the reasons children are not allowed to eat all of their Halloween candy before midnight on Halloween. It is also one of the reasons God gave parents – to protect their children from themselves. Children are inexperienced and need good, mature guidance from someone who loves them.

As we grow older, we should also mature (I Cor. 13.11). The problem is, no matter how mature and experienced we become, there is someone out there smarter and more worldly-wise than we. When they speak, they lead to destruction and their flattery sweetens the path that leads to a fall.

We cannot fully prepare ourselves for every flattering word or every sweet offer, but we can prepare our hearts. Someone once said, "The greatest thought I've ever had is: 'Jesus loves me, this I know.'" God loves you. What an absolutely awesome thought. His ways are perfect and He would never lead those He loves in paths of destruction.

Uncommon Praises from Common Psalms

Because of God's great love, we can pray without reservation: *"Lead me, O LORD, in thy righteousness because of mine enemies; make thy way straight before my face."*

It is not necessary to understand the reason – it is sufficient to know God cares.

The Bass in God's Choir

"To the chief Musician on Neginoth upon Sheminith, A Psalm of David. O LORD, rebuke me not in thine anger, neither chasten me in thy hot displeasure." Psalm 6.1

This psalm begins with musical instructions for its performance. Neginoth suggests that it is to be played on stringed instruments and also that it is a psalm of taunting. As you read through this passage you will see abundant evidence that this is the intent because David is weeping, groaning and generally worn out from his predicament. It is also to be a song upon Sheminith – a word whose root means eight or octave. Believing that this suggests a musical octave, the music would be low rather than high; after all, the higher lilting songs were sung by the Alamoth (Temple virgins – a young girls' choir).

Most of us would rather live in the upper spiritual sphere where the sweet notes of the young girls blend in antiphonal tones that both please the ear and calm the heart. From those melodic passages we worship and praise as naturally as the song birds sing; however, in that frame of mind we learn very little of ourselves and even less of the greatness of God.

We experience the bass in Gospel quartets, symphony orchestras, pipe organs, and even in the thunder. The bass reverberates throughout the hall even penetrating floors and walls. It affects us as nothing else can. It will not be ignored.

The bass enters and begins to sing; his voice is so low that we can almost count the vibrations. It is a voice that we cannot escape because we can feel its affect. This is the voice David felt as he wrote this psalm. He was no more ready to "whistle while he worked" than he was to "sing in the rain." He was down – low in spirit – hurting all the way to his bones (verse 2). He had wept until there were no more tears and had mourned until there was nothing left in him (verse 6).

Uncommon Praises from Common Psalms

About 3:30 this morning I reached across the bed and took my wife's hand in mine. I thought she was asleep. She was awake; she squeezed my hand. Without thinking, I asked her, "Do you ever think of where Mandy would be if she was still alive?" Without hesitation she answered, "Every day." The bass became more profound and vibrated me – to my soul. As my eyes watered, I thought to myself that after nearly twelve years it would seem that the bass would not vibrate quite so violently.

So often when the bass gets turned up, we run to escape it. It is not so pleasant when it rocks our world. But just as the bass is the foundation for good composition, we would be incomplete without it in our lives. Although we need to praise, we also need to weep. In weeping we learn so much more about God and about ourselves.

Because of the bass notes, I learned about prayer (among other things) – not just saying a prayer, and not just asking for things from God; but true prayer – communion with God. The God who sticks closer than a brother. The God who listens anytime and responds in love. The God who loves me more than anyone. The God who allows the bass notes in my life so I can feel the need to cast my every care upon Him. This is the God who sometimes rattles your cage in order to get your attention. Never run from the bass notes in your life; run to God. Seek shelter under His Almighty presence. Accept the safe haven He offers. Then the bass notes complete the harmony rather than disrupt the calm.

(Mandy was our daughter who was killed in a car accident in December of 1998.)

How to Treat Your Enemy

"If I have rewarded evil unto him that was at peace with me; (yea, I have delivered him that without cause is mine enemy:..." Psalm 7.4

Being nice to nice people has never been much of a challenge. Even when you wake up in a mood, a friendly, kind voice tends to lighten up the day. But what about all those out there who wake in a mood as low as yours? What about those who just simply don't like you?

This is another of David's plaintiff psalms, but with a twist. Although it may be difficult to put a firm meaning on the word "Shiggaion," there is enough background to indicate that it refers to something with wide variation – a rambling poem.

David has caught himself in succumbing to his emotions rather than rising above them. Rather than speaking kindly of those who persecuted him, he found himself caught by the same evil that he abhorred. The emotional roller-coaster he is on causes him to fluctuate between praising God and abhorring himself. He cries out to God as his defense and sinks into slander as a means of self-preservation.

I learned long ago (at least intellectually more so than in application) that I can learn as much or more from my enemies than from my friends. I do not minimize the friendship and fellowship of friends, but enemies will tell you things you do not want to hear. Enemies are not kind and do not mince words. While a friend will try to soothe and often sugar coat the truth; the enemy does none of that – he will not spare your feelings. To accept the praise of friends and dismiss the barbs of the enemy simply because of a good or bad relationship is to deny oneself a proper exercise of God-given wisdom.

Saul was in many respects the enemy. The words he hurled at David were vicious and hurtful, but David neither discounted the messenger nor the message. He looked carefully at the accusation. "If I have...Let the enemy..." In the end, David could, with a clear

Uncommon Praises from Common Psalms

conscience, turn his case over to the Lord. (Psalm 7.17) He had heard the accusations; he had considered the words; and he had submitted it to God.

If you have no enemies, you are fortunate. That is not the case with most people. Although we cannot stop people from being our enemies and we have no control over what they say about us, we do have control over how we respond. When the enemy shoots hurtful barbs our way, we should take a hard look at ourselves and determine whether any were deserved. If they are deserved, we should repent quickly. If they are not deserved, we should not be overcome with emotional trauma, but rather trust the problem to the One who cares.

Arrogance and Judgment

"When I consider thy heavens, the work of thy fingers, the moon and the stars, which thou hast ordained, What is man, that thou art mindful of him? and the son of man, that thou visitest him?" Psalm 8.3, 4

Some years ago Russian cosmonauts when to the edge of our space, looked around, and declared that there was no God because they could not see Him. Since I have never personally been that far up, I have no information base upon which to compare my life experience with theirs.

As a matter of fact, there are many things about which I know very little or nothing. For example, I have never seen a strand of DNA through a microscope. I have also never seen (with my own eyes up close and in person) a duck billed platypus. I assume these things exist because reputable scientists verify the existence of the DNA and photographs corroborate the stories of the odd-looking animal.

For anyone to say that something does not exist simply because they have not seen it or experienced it suggests that they have a complete and flawless knowledge base (i.e. They know everything there is to know.). To suggest that miracles do not occur because of a lack of personal experience suggests that the entire universe rests within that person's knowledge base – that nothing can be known outside of that individual's knowledge.

The ultimate expression of arrogance is to state with conviction that there is no God. It is the fool who denies the existence of God. (Psalm 14.1) Can that degree of arrogance even be imagined? I think not!

Psalm 8 is addressed *"To the Chief Musician upon Gittith."* "Gittith" is a word that means "winepress." Winepresses have always been a symbol of judgment. Judgment by God will not be based upon how high you scored on achievement tests or even how much you accomplish in society. Judgment will be based upon what you do about God, and more specifically upon what you do about Jesus the Christ.

Uncommon Praises from Common Psalms

In order for humans (who happen to be specks on a dot in the vast universe) to understand that there is a God, He placed the moon and the stars to draw our attention skyward. He also "visited" us in order to show us the only way by which we can have a personal relationship with Him.

Who are we that God's attention should be drawn toward us? We are they who, without His intervention, would live and die in our arrogance thinking we are the world – never knowing our desperate need for salvation.

When we consider God, our hearts should break out in a grand refrain as did the Psalmist's: *"O LORD our Lord, how excellent is thy name in all the earth!" (Psalm 8.9)*

A Matter of Perspective

"The LORD also will be a refuge for the oppressed, a refuge in times of trouble." Psalm 9.9

My crew of officials and I entered the pitch (soccer field) at Wando High School for a match between the Warriors and the Summerville High School Green Wave. We began our pre-game check of the field, players, and other equipment. As it is prior to the start of any game, there is some time to walk the field – checking things so as to remove as many surprises as possible – becoming acquainted with our surroundings.

Wando High School (the old campus) is located near the coast. Its field is lighted by four very tall light towers (well over 100 feet tall) – each bearing a bank of lights and a small runway on which workers can safely stand to change lights. I say "safely" because that is way too high for me and I would feel unsafe after reaching the third or fourth rung of the ladder. I will not admit to being afraid of heights, just that I really enjoy having my feet on the ground.

I have always admired people who work at great heights – envied them at times for how they can scale light towers or radio towers with little or no fear. I watch as they get smaller as they move higher.

Just before the start of the match, I looked up and saw an osprey gliding toward one of the towers carrying a fish in its mouth. I had missed it – there on the runway was an enormous nest. Although I could not see inside the nest (and had no thoughts of scaling the tower) I could see the osprey standing on the edge of the nest tending to some young ones.

A natural sight – the osprey is not only fearless of the heights, but seeks them out. That is what it does by nature. For me, on the other hand, seeking the heights would be unnatural.

The psalmist uses the word "refuge" meaning: "height, a high place of defense and protection." The Lord is the believer's high tower –

Uncommon Praises from Common Psalms

his rock and fortress. Just as the osprey seeks its aerie for safety, so the believer seeks the Lord for protection.

It is natural for the believer to run to the Lord – to the Lord's people – to the Lord's house. Having a new nature by being a new creation in Christ changes the natural tendencies of an individual. No longer does the believer seek refuge in the world and its vanities. While the unbeliever escapes to the mountains, the beach, and often the bottle; the believer escapes to the refuge from which the unbeliever flees – the Lord Jesus Christ.

We should take a close look at our tendencies – our habits of flight. When in difficult circumstances, which direction do you run? Do you run toward Christ or away? Do you cling tightly to Him or to things of the world?

Standing One's Ground

"He hath said in his heart, I shall not be moved: for I shall never be in adversity." Psalm 10.6

Arrogance has no bounds. That part of a person's belief system seems to be associated with their view of the world around them and how they believe they fit into it.

For example, in the world of sports a common chant is, "We're number one!" So zealously they shout it that it's almost believable – at least until the other team gets onto the field. I have seen teams who have been utterly routed, and while the scoreboard shows their terrible defeat the cheerleaders and fans are shouting to the top of their lungs, "We're number one!" Remember that there can only be one number one.

I suppose the fire ant thinks of his world as being all there is – to this little creature this is the center of the universe. The colony of small creatures builds their nests under the ground – in their own world, leaving the signs of their success above the ground in another world. If you inadvertently step on their mound, you will experience their wrath; however, just as inadvertently a lawn mower may clip the top of their domain and cause quite a scurry, disrupting their very existence.

From the human's perspective (the one causing the problems for the ants), the ant is a tiny, insignificant creature that is more a nuisance than an integral part of the world. The human looks down, feels a bit superior and in control as he drops some poison on the mound to rid his lawn of the pest. He is in control. He stands with great pride that he has once again conquered his territory.

It seems not to matter what your domain happens to be; we all tend to express the same arrogance in some way or another. "This is my car." "This is my life; you won't tell me how to live it." "This is my house. You will live by my rules." "You can't tell me what to do." "I'm in charge – you will answer to me and do as I say!"

Uncommon Praises from Common Psalms

Do any of those sound familiar? The ant believes he is the greatest. The mom or dad believes he is the greatest. The husband believes he is the greatest. The prize fighter believes he is the greatest. The company CEO believes he is the greatest. The dictator believes he is the greatest. And, it goes on. This is the spirit of antichrist – to be in charge of one's life with no restrictions – in submission to no one. The "great one" stands before God with his fist raised in defiance saying, "This is my domain; you can't move me!"

Tragically, we make our own domain and live in it without considering there is Someone greater than we. At the top of this world's future history, a man will arise who will be the supreme dictator of the world – ruling the greatest possible domain ever conceived of by human definition; however, there is Someone above that.

"The LORD is King for ever and ever: the heathen are perished out of his land." (Psalm 10.16)

No matter how arrogantly someone stands within their own domain, God is greater. At some point in the future, every knee shall bow before the King of kings and Lord of lords. (Romans 14.11) It behooves each of us to submit our domain to the One who is truly in charge – the One who has the victory already won – the One who can both show us the perfect way to live and the perfect way to eternal life.

Foundations

"If the foundations be destroyed, what can the righteous do?" Psalm 11.3

There has never been a more urgent need for proper foundations. Foundations are those things upon which the superstructures of life are erected. Without a proper foundation, there is no stability and certainly no integrity of structure.

In ever sports rule book, there is a chapter on definitions. Unless an official knows the definition of a "horse-collar" tackle, his enforcement of the rule will be, at best, hap-hazard. Unless an official knows when a player becomes a shooter, he cannot properly and consistently enforce a penalty awarding free throws.

Many people have gone away from the foundations of the Christian faith. While many still use the name Jesus, that name may not mean what the Bible expresses. A recent fad of wearing a WWJD wrist band was a statement – but, not everyone was saying the same thing. It is not uncommon at our church for young people to come to our Wednesday teen groups or children's ministries who have only heard the name Jesus used as an expletive.

So, who is Jesus?

The Bible states with conviction that He is the "Word" of God who was in the beginning with God. (John 1.1-5) It further states that He is God manifested in the flesh – co-existent and co-equal in every respect with the Father and Spirit (John 10.30, *"one" = "of one essence, one and the same"*). The expression "was in the beginning with God" requires the Jesus was already there, not that He was the first of Creation. Paul writes and expresses the fact that all creation was brought about by Him (Colossians 1.16, 17)

Not only is/was He God; but, He became (was made) flesh. (John 1.14) The author of Hebrews expresses this clearly when he writes, *"a body hast thou prepared me."* (Hebrews 10.5) Thus, Jesus was not the "only Son" or the "unique Son" (as some modern translations maintain), but He was the "only begotten" Son of God.

Uncommon Praises from Common Psalms

The word "begotten" carries the idea of being physically born. That is exactly what happened when the Holy Spirit came upon Mary and she conceived (Luke 1.35) – Jesus was physically conceived and was born. Jesus, God from eternity past, received a body of flesh through which He would perform the work of the Sacrificial Lamb – the shedding of His blood in payment for sin.

This foundational truth is only one of many required for a proper understanding of the Bible. When Jesus said, "I am the way, the truth, and the life, no man cometh unto the Father but by me" (John 14.6), that is exactly what He meant. When Luke recorded the words, "Neither is there salvation in any other: for there is none other name under heaven given among men whereby we must be saved" (Acts 4.12), that is exactly what he meant.

Smudging foundational truths into a dingy gray only weakens the structure of the Gospel. When discussing Jesus, lay proper foundations – know of whom you speak. Accept no fuzzy conversations, but stand firmly on the foundational truths of God's Word.

Much Ado About Nothing

"They speak vanity every one with his neighbour: with flattering lips and with a double heart do they speak." Psalm 12.2

The word "vanity" means, "emptiness, vanity, or falsehood." It is from a root meaning smooth and was used of Jacob's skin as compared to Esau's (who was an outdoor's man).

When I was about eight years old, I missed the first three days of vacation Bible school because of an illness. By the time I made it to craft class on Thursday, all of the class was way ahead of me and many had nearly finished their project. The project was a cross-stitch pattern of a heart and cross that we were to sew on a piece of screen wire rather than cross-stitch cloth.

My attempt to finish the project was hurried and sloppy. Our craft lady told me it was nice – considering I had been sick and gave it to me to take home on Friday. When my mother saw it, she informed me that I would take out every stitch and re-sew it properly. Her comment was, "Anything worth doing is worth doing right." I tried to tell her I had been sick, but she would hear none of that.

It is now 45 plus years later. The lesson my mother taught me still rings in my ears today. It causes me to want to do my best in everything I attempt – to study hard and to be diligent. Failure is not a bad thing when the failure is corrected. If proper instruction follows, failures become our greatest tools for learning.

Psalm 12.2 is nothing more than ancient words for the modern "self-esteem" movement where no one is allowed to fail and anything done is acceptable. Parents, teachers, preachers, and especially counselors are afraid to bruise a little guy's ego. They will pacify him with words and pills. He will most often grow into an old child who knows nothing of problem solving and providing for a family – a child who expects the world to care for his every need and make him feel good about himself.

Uncommon Praises from Common Psalms

In reality, flattery (building one's self-esteem rather than equipping someone to achieve) is one of the greatest banes in society – it destroys true worth and value in an individual. It dulls ones motivation to excel and be the best at the thing God has gifted them to do. It is in fact an insult because it kills an individual's drive to do well.

Sound, Bible preaching churches have a difficult job these days. The Bible does not flatter. It calls us what we are – sinners in need of a Savior. Society has driven the church into the modern era of pacifying Junior. The service is built around a "feel-good" philosophy so when people leave they are no longer introspective, but rather they feel no need to change from a sinful life. So long as everything is "smooth" all is right with the world.

Psalm 12.6 says, "The words of the LORD are pure words: as silver tried in a furnace of earth, purified seven times." Because His words are pure and true, when He says, "Good job," it is really a good job. For those who faithfully serve Him, His words will be *"Well done, good and faithful servant; thou hast been faithful over a few things, I will make thee ruler over many things: enter thou into the joy of thy lord."* (Matthew 25.21, 23)

Always do your best – God will bless.

Patience

How long wilt thou forget me, O LORD? for ever? how long wilt thou hide thy face from me? How long shall I take counsel in my soul, having sorrow in my heart daily? how long shall mine enemy be exalted over me? Psalm 13.1, 2

One Sunday morning while the husband was in the car waiting impatiently, (intermittently laying on the horn) his wife appeared at the doorway with a half-clad baby in her arms. She leaned through the door and yelled, "How about you coming inside and finish getting the baby ready and let me honk the horn a while!"

We have all from time-to-time become impatient. During most road trips, the children's favorite question is: "Are we there yet?" Even the ability to wait patiently for Christmas morning to arrive for the opening of presents increases with maturity. As we grow and mature, our patience level should increase – I say should because some people simply grow older without maturing.

A mark of true maturity is one's ability to trust those of greater maturity. When I was a small child, I would wait only because my Dad told me to wait and I knew the consequences for being openly impatient. On the outside I was waiting, but on the inside I was a bundle of nervous energy ready to spring.

In life there are many situations, people, and environmental problems that test our patience. When carefully considered, our ability to be patient in and through the problem rests upon our ability to trust. By trusting in self, we are limiting our ability to handle the situation. By being impatient with God, we limit our ability to see His awesome hand in working things out for the best. (We also show our lack of trust by our impatience.)

Once we have done all we can do and exhausted all available options, there is nothing left to do but to be patient and watch God work. Haven't you marveled when you have observed how wonderfully God works things out? Hasn't it amazed you to see what God has done by answering in a fashion you never dreamed

Uncommon Praises from Common Psalms

of? We should be quick to remember that man's extremity is God's opportunity.

He is still the same God – He is faithful when things are good and when they are bad. The same God who answered decisively in the past is the same God who will amaze you with your current problem. Be patient – God is working.

The Fool

"The fool hath said in his heart, There is no God." Psalm 14.1a

Because my father's work place was near our elementary school (and because I loathed riding the school bus), he would take my brother and me to school in the mornings. This may sound as strange to you as it did to me at the time, but the last words my father would say while we were getting out of his 64 Chevy pickup were, "Be smart." Not "Be careful," or "Be good," but "Be smart."

Although that baffled me for many years, I believe I finally have a handle on what he meant.

Most of my life has been dedicated to teaching. If any of my teachers are out there reading this, please don't have heart failure when I say that I really enjoy studying. I really enjoy learning truths that I had not previously known. I delight in solving questions and having answers.

That alone does not make someone smart nor does it keep someone from being a fool.

One of my pet peeves is when someone asks a question and then argues with the answer. If you want an answer, accept it. If you don't want an answer, don't ask it. But, to ask someone for an answer only to argue with the answer is futile at best and foolish at least.

So what does all this have to do with "being smart?" Being smart implies not only a good, working knowledge of facts, but it also implies the ability to apply those facts in practical applications (a definition of wisdom). Being smart suggests that a person is open to instruction and is willing to change when previously unknown truth is introduced. Being a fool implies just the opposite – having such strong opinions that the truth cannot bring about change.

"The fool hath said in his heart, There is no God." The fool ignores instruction from those who are wiser and more experienced. The

Uncommon Praises from Common Psalms

fool hears truth but disregards it. The fool has access to truth but does not apply it to his life. In essence, the fool is not being smart. How foolish it is to hear truth from the Creator God, written in His Word to us, and not apply it personally to our lives. How foolish it is to know what God says, and walk away without taking care to obey it in every particular. It is as if we have walked into His presence, asked a question, and then argued with His answer.

Some mornings when I ready myself for the day, I can almost hear my father say, "Be smart." When I have my daily moments with my Lord, I can almost hear Him say, "Be smart."

As you prepare yourself for the day, take the advice of a loving Father and "Be smart."

Communion

"LORD, who shall abide in thy tabernacle? Who shall dwell in thy holy hill?"
Psalm 15.1

Nearly every Friday night during football season, a select group of individuals make their way to a meeting place. These individuals are properly referred to as football officials (although some use other terms of endearment). Even though we are required to be at the pre-game site at least one and one-half hours before kickoff, the veteran officials see the value in arriving long before that. It is not uncommon for officials to arrive two or three hours early.

For some of us, preparation for what we do on Friday nights began as early in the year as March and April. That's when the books come out and the studying begins in earnest. We want to learn as much as possible so that when we get to the pre-game conference and later arrive on the field, we are on the same page and thinking the same thoughts.

Those who arrive early have time to escape from the day's hectic pace and settle in for some "down time" before shifting into high gear for the scheduled contest. During that time, the game officials prepare their minds and attitudes and also acquaint themselves with the other officials (We sometimes work with officials we meet for the first time at this pre-game conference.)

We discuss specific coverage areas, special situations (i.e. on-side kick coverage, etc.), rules changes, and other items of importance. In other words, we prepare for the game long before the game begins.

When a crew of officials walks onto the football field, we are of one mind. How often have you seen game officials arguing with each other? There are sometimes arguments with coaches and fans, but not with each other.

In the above verse, two words arrest my attention: "abide" and "dwell." "Abide" speaks of a sojourner who is walking with and in

Uncommon Praises from Common Psalms

fellowship with his companion. Amos asks the question, *"Can two walk together, except they be agreed?"* (Amos 3.3) In order for anyone to abide together, there must be agreement – and that must be based upon understanding and understanding is based upon communication and time spent together. "Dwell" has a more permanent connotation. While it does not take away from the abiding, it adds the thought of a permanent enjoyment and fellowship – a staying together because of unity of hearts and minds.

Have you ever taken time to notice how rushed people are on Sunday mornings? Those who come early and stay late are like the veteran officials – they are there because they really enjoy what they are doing – the fellowship and preparation for the up-coming contest (life outside church). Long before the singing or the start of the sermon, their hearts and minds are prepared – ready for worship. Those who slip in late and leave immediately often retort that the church is either unfriendly or cold.

How tragic it is that we must "pump people up" before we can begin our worship and praise. How difficult it is to *"be still and know that I am God"* (Psalm 46.10), when our hearts have barely slowed from the mad dash from parking lot to pew.

My parents often reminded me that anything worth doing is worth doing right. Don't you think praising and worshipping God is worth it? If we can spend time preparing for jobs, games, meals, and family reunions, doesn't it stand to reason that if we really want to walk with God, we should spend time preparing ourselves? Who can abide and dwell with the Lord? Those who think it is worth being prepared.

Security Blankets

"The LORD is the portion of mine inheritance and of my cup: thou maintainest my lot." Psalm 16.5

One of the icons associated with the "Peanuts" cartoon is Linus holding his security blanket. Quite often the playful Snoopy flashes by and swipes the blanket leaving Linus holding nothing – no security and no sympathy. Charlie Brown is unsympathetic and Lucy is cynical.

None of us enjoys admitting it, but we all have our security blankets. Think not? How did you react when your wife took your "favorite" sweatshirt to Good Will? Not very logical on her part – it only had a few holes and a couple of permanent stains. But, it was comfortable. It was full of memories.

The late Vance Havner once said, "When I began this road of life everyone I loved was on this side of eternity. After many years of travel, most have crossed over to the other side making the prospects of heaven sweeter."*

There are times when God takes away our security blankets so we can see the big picture, eternity, more clearly. Although we cherish our wedding pictures, a vintage automobile, a special t-shirt, and our loved ones; those things sometimes becomes our security blanket – a security blanket that keeps us from clinging tightly to our God.

The phrase "the portion of mine inheritance" is something of a play on words in the Hebrew. It suggests the idea of "the part that I hold dear out of what has been given to me" – that part that gives me comfort when I am low and lonely. The psalmist's security blanket is the LORD (Jehovah – the Savior).

Not only is He a soft blanket for cradling our weary hearts, but He is our "cup" of hot cocoa when we are cold. Linus could only hold his blanket and suck his thumb; but, the believer can rest

Uncommon Praises from Common Psalms

confidently in his Savior and enjoy an overflowing cup of refreshment (Psalm 23.5).

Our security blankets give us comfort so long as we have them, but our God secures us forever because He "maintainest {our} lot {future, destiny}."

What, then, is your security blanket? A beach house? A cabin at the lake? Mom? Dad? Your education? Your job?

None of those last forever in this world. Remember, only Jesus can satisfy completely and eternally. Make the LORD your portion so that your lot is secure and your cup filled to overflowing.

*(The quotation by Vance Havner is from memory and is not verbatim; it does however offer the essence of its content.)

Innocent Perspective

"Thou hast proved mine heart; thou hast visited me in the night; thou hast tried me, and shalt find nothing; I am purposed that my mouth shall not transgress."
Psalm 17.3

Some of us remember the "good old days" (that actually were no better or worse than today) when school teachers needed to remind us that the word "Principal" ended with the word "pal." While there were some kids who actually enjoyed going to the Principal's office, I was not one of them.

Everyone knew that the Principal had secret "weapons" that he used on students just to satisfy his sadistic appetite. During sixth grade the class bully, Harold, was called to the Principal's office for some mischief he had created. Upon Harold's return, he reported that the Principal had strapped him to a table and set the "electric paddle" to the highest level, shut the door, and left the room. It must have been true because Harold had returned to class with red, tear-stained eyes.

Later that year, I was called to the principal's office. The office was across campus (about 100 yards or so). The trek took forever. It seemed a barren desert as I plodded along – getting ever closer and not wanting to be there. With every step the anxiety grew as I combed my brain trying to think of what I had done to deserve this call. Whatever it was, it must have been terrible. Would the Principal use the electric paddle or would he choose to use the one with the holes drilled in it?

With all my deep soul searching, I could think of nothing – nothing worthy of such a sentence at such a young age. I had my whole life ahead of me.

As I pushed open the door our Principal was standing inside waiting. He looked so big – so austere. Then he smiled and stretched out his hand. I winced, shied back, trying to avoid whatever lay ahead. The Principal reached out took my hand in a warm shake, put his hand on my shoulder and told me I had been

Uncommon Praises from Common Psalms

selected to help out with the lunch detail. (That included free lunch and extra dessert.) Even though I was relieved, my knees went limp as I sat in the nearest chair.

David was facing problems all around and taking his problems to God. As he approached God, he searched his heart – deeply – to insure his innocence. It was not enough to consider himself to be innocent; most people are able to arrange facts so that they either justify their actions or excuse themselves from guilt. But, David looked deep within from God's perspective.

Notice the three tests he used. 1) Proved – "examine, scrutinize," 2) Visited – "attend, search out," and 3) Tried – "refine, purify." Not only had David considered carefully his position, but he knew God had also taken notice. Nothing is hidden from God. He knows our heart and our actions – motives and works.

While we may be able to pull the wool over the eyes of our Principal, boss, wife, etc., there is never any wool over the eyes of the Almighty. Many seem to use their prayer time to meet with God to justify their actions and attitudes. No one has ever been made righteous while attempting self-justification. Righteousness (a right relationship) is accomplished only as we come clean, confessing our wrong.

Before coming into His presence with singing, we must first examine ourselves – thoroughly examine ourselves. During that long walk across the campus, determine what is needed to correct our lives before we meet with our Father. When He opens the door, be ready with a meek and contrite heart. Know that there is nothing amiss between you and God. Then, enjoy the fellowship.

The Rock

"The LORD is my rock, and my fortress, and my deliverer; my God, my strength, in whom I will trust; my buckler, and the horn of my salvation, and my high tower." Psalm 18.2

My father and his family moved from Stokes County, NC during his early adult life. One of the reasons for the move was that, along with being a blacksmith, my grandfather was a farmer. The fields in Stokes County were littered with rocks – rocks from golf ball size to larger than a basketball. The locals called them "flint rocks." (They were actually quartz – number seven on the hardness scale.) There seemed to be an endless supply of rocks that oozed from parts unknown to the surface of the fields to wreak havoc on the good intentions of the farmer.

Each year the field had to be cleared – manually – by backbreaking labor. Each year rocks resurfaced making field preparation nearly impossible – often frustrating the efforts of the farmer.

Just down the road from my grandfather my great-uncle (my grandmother's brother) built his log cabin. The rocks caused problems in the fields as well as in the ground when trying to dig a foundation ditch. As Uncle Miller prepared the foundation, he dug out the rocks – but he did not leave them out. After all, there are few things that make a better foundation for a home than a rock.

The rocks from the digging and the rocks from the field were used to give Uncle Miller's and Aunt Percy's log cabin a sure footing. Those rocks were laid upon the bedrock of the mountain; arranged in a fashion that would ensure a solid place upon which to build. Even when they added on to the cabin, the original foundation was still holding firm. As a matter of fact, the foundation is still holding firm today.

Buildings are no better than the foundation upon which they are erected. An individual's character is no different; it is only as good as the foundation upon which it is based.

Uncommon Praises from Common Psalms

In the midst of perilous times, it is reassuring to know that "The LORD is my rock."

It is not always easy for a Christian to maintain his proper focus and attitude due to the rocky fields of life, but each of those rocks help make the believer stronger as we use experiences interpreted through the eyes of our Savior and God.

The very things that cause us anguish and discomfort – even heartache and pain – when placed upon the Rock, become blessings that will support us in life. The rocks that cause the field to be unusable are foundational stones upon which we build the superstructure of a mature, spiritual life – a life founded upon the sure Foundation.

Whenever rocks appear in your field, gather them together and use them positively, laying them on the Rock of your salvation, as you construct the edifice of your character.

Remember, *"He brought me up also out of an horrible pit, out of the miry clay, and set my feet upon a rock, and established my goings."* (Psalm 40:2)

Sunday Mouth

"Let the words of my mouth, and the meditation of my heart, be acceptable in thy sight, O LORD, my strength, and my redeemer." Psalm 19.14

I arrived early for my football game in Beaufort, SC to find that one of my partners, Skip, an umpire, who I had never met before, had already arrived. We had some time to get acquainted and enjoyed the fact that both of us were believers. As we shared our faith with each other, recounting some of the blessings of God in our lives, a trio of other officials barged through the doors quite oblivious to the fact that we were there.

One was in the middle of telling a rather off-colored joke. Skip raised an index finger motioning for me to hold my peace – which I did. Since I had never met any of these officials either, when the joke was done, Skip introduced me by saying, "Let me introduce you to Reverend Hill" – with an emphasis on the "Reverend" part.

Amazingly enough, the jokester reddened and began listing his duties at his church. It seems he was a choir member, a Sunday school teacher, and an Elder. In a situation like that, it is quite difficult to stay one's mind and heart from forming some opinions.

It is sad indeed to realize that this "Christian" is probably not the only one out there who has a different language on Sunday than during the rest of the week. How is it that on Sunday we can sing praise to the Almighty God and speak of fellowship with our Lord when on Monday He seems to have faded into the background?

How is it that come Monday, our high exaltation of His presence during our praise and worship time melds with the work-a-day world and our life becomes less than holy? And our hallowed greetings on Sundays with brothers and sisters in Christ become the topics of conversational gossip during breaks on Mondays?

God's Word requires that our language and our musings be acceptable ("be pleasurable") in the sight of ("before the face of")

Uncommon Praises from Common Psalms

our Savior who is our strength ("solid rock") and our redeemer ("kinsman redeemer").

Do we speak two languages? Do we speak the same language on Sunday as on Monday? Would our Savior and God be pleased with us every time we open our mouth and speak?

Oh, did I mention attitudes?

Offering or Sacrifice?

"Remember all thy offerings, and accept thy burnt sacrifice; Selah." Psalm 20.3

Someone has described the difference between an offering and a sacrifice by observing a Southern breakfast table. While the chicken gave an offering (the egg), the pig made a sacrifice (the bacon).

Mandy broke into the world as most babies do – startled by the light and more startled by the swift swat on her backside to get her breathing. It was a most incredible sight. When she turned blue, a nurse quickly took her from the room to "pink her up" a little. She was born with double pneumonia and needed some oxygen.

During the next few days in the intensive care unit, she stopped breathing three times. With monitors, sensors, and needles all around her body, she was not the prettiest sight I had seen; however, she stole my heart.

Mandy was bright – the apple of her father's eye.

On December 19, 1998, her physical life was taken in an automobile accident – six days before Christmas. She was 15 years old.

Just the other day, Nancy and I were reminiscing about Mandy. I asked her, "If you could, would you bring her back?" In a word, my wife expressed my own sentiments, "No." Please don't misunderstand – there is not a day that goes by when we don't miss her and often our eyes fill with tears when we think of her, but we would not have her back.

Before Mandy was born, Nancy and I had offered her to God. When she was a baby, we dedicated her to God – offering her to Him – placing her in His loving arms – asking for His will to be accomplished in her life. Mandy had received God's gift of salvation offered through the shed blood of the Lord Jesus Christ. His decision was to remove her from our care into His own.

Uncommon Praises from Common Psalms

In every aspect of our lives we must ask the question, *"Shall not the Judge of all the earth do right?"* (Genesis 18.25) Did we make an offering or did we make a sacrifice? An offering may be made without complete commitment, but a sacrifice involves commitment. A sacrifice causes us to take our hands completely off the thing (or person) offered and causes us to place our unquestioning trust in the hands of another.

When you drop your offering in the church collection plate, do you have strings attached? When your children are not following the path you think is right, do you trust God with their correction? When your child wants to be a missionary to the jungles of the Amazon, can you let go and allow God to lead him?

So, have you made an offering or a sacrifice? If you have dedicated your life to your Savior, have you placed your life completely in His hands – including family, finances, and friends? If God chose to take something from you, would you live in self-pity over the loss as Jonah (Jonah 4.9), or would you rejoice that God found you worthy of His attention? (Philippians 3.7)

The answer to Abraham's question, *"Shall not the Judge of all the earth do right?"* is a resounding "YES!"

Career or Calling

"For thou hast made him most blessed for ever: thou hast made him exceeding glad with thy countenance. For the king trusteth in the LORD, and through the mercy of the most High he shall not be moved." Psalm 21.6, 7

I remember the first Guidance Counselor that came to our school. She arrived at the beginning of my freshman year in high school. It was her job to help point students toward a field of work in which they had interest or aptitude.

From the age of twelve, I knew the career God wanted for me so I never went to the Guidance Counselor even though many of my friends did. That is a bit early in life I know, but I believed God wanted me to be a pastor – not a missionary, evangelist, etc. – but a pastor.

I use the term "career" intentionally, because that is the work that I do. Most probably your career is different; if we all did the same thing; there would be no variety in the world.

David's career as a shepherd changed abruptly when the prophet anointed him to be king over Israel. That was a radical career change. Although he became king, his shepherd's heart did not change.

While most of us have different careers, and often our careers change, if you are a child of God, we all have the same calling. That calling is to be "conformed to the image of his Son {Jesus Christ}."

The point is this: the most important part of your life is not your career, it is your calling. Careers may change, but your calling does not. You may retire from your career, but you never retire from your calling. Your calling may get in the way of your career, but your career should never get in the way of your calling.

By carefully studying the life of David, the student need not go far to find lapses in David's faithfulness. Each time David fell, it was because he put his career ahead of his calling. As he stood on the

Uncommon Praises from Common Psalms

roof of his palace, he looked out and saw a woman bathing on the next building. Had he kept his calling ahead of his career, his fall would have never happened.

Whenever our career eclipses our calling we are in danger.

The first phrase of the above verse, "For thou hast made him most blessed for ever..." literally means that God had caused David to be a blessing to others. When David considered his career as a means to an end and not an end in itself, he blessed others. When David considered career as more important than his calling, he brought shame upon God's people.

Careers are important because they allow us to earn money so that we can fulfill our calling. Too often, however, we become so engrossed with our career that we abandon that which is most important – our calling of God. Maybe we should take a closer look. Check to see which is most important. A good test is this: do you miss work to serve Christ, or do you miss ministry opportunities to be at work? Do you hoard the money God has blessed you with, or do you use it for the expansion of His kingdom? Remember that your career is for life, but your calling is for eternity.

We bless others as we are true to our calling not because we spend more hours in the office.

The Worm

"But I am a worm, and no man; a reproach of men, and despised of the people." Psalm 22.6

The three Psalms before us form a trilogy of truth concerning our Shepherd. Psalm 22 speaks of the Good Shepherd who gives His life for His sheep. Psalm 23 speaks of the Great Shepherd who cares for His sheep. And Psalm 24 speaks of the Chief Shepherd who lives for His sheep.

Some believe that Jesus, while on the cross, quoted Psalm 22 in its entirety even though we have only a few lines recorded for us in the Gospels. Matthew records the words of the suffering Savior, "My God, My God, why hast thou forsaken me." (Psalm 22.1; Matthew 27.46) There is also the great and final declaration of Psalm 22.31, "that he hath done this," which literally means, "What he has finished!" John's recording of it is in the Greek, τετελεσται (tetelestai) meaning, "It is finished!"

Throughout this psalm, however, is a detailed account of our Savior's sufferings. Those sufferings are summed up in verse six. After having taken upon Himself our sin, the Savior viewed Himself as "a worm, and no{t a} man." He was a "reproach of men, and despised of the people."

The worm, tola, was a despicable creature – a maggot, a red grub that fed upon the repulsive rottenness of refuse. This was the worm that infested the rotted manna (Exodus 16.20) and that feasted upon the cankered sores of Job (Job 25.6). This is the worm that deprived Jonah of his shade provided by God's grace through the gourd (Jonah 4.7). Despised and loathed, this worm would cause the hearty soul to turn squeamish.

As the Savior of the world hung on the cross – bruised, beaten, and battered beyond recognition, bearing the sins of the entire world – even his mother was repulsed by the sight (John 19.26, 27). Thank God in His marvelous foreknowledge and wisdom, the Savior did not remain a repulsive human spectacle.

Uncommon Praises from Common Psalms

It is quite worth noting that the word translated "worm" (tola) is used 42 times in the Old Testament. Thirty-three times it is translated "scarlet," and once it is translated "crimson." It is thus translated because of the attributes the worm produced in its death. The worm was a crimson color. When crushed it produced an extremely expensive dye used to color cloth worn only by royalty.

It was imperative that our Savior be crushed (Isaiah 53) and die in order to provide salvation for humanity. It was imperative that our Savior bear our sins in His own body on the cross. It was imperative that our Savior shed His precious blood – for without the shedding of blood there is no remission of sins. (Matthew 26.28, Hebrews 9.22)

The One who was despised and rejected of men bled blood sufficient enough for the sins of all who believe on Him. There is provision enough through Christ's shed blood to provide crimson garments to clothe all God's children. But only God's children are permitted to wear these garments. Only God's children are heirs of God's riches and joint-heirs with Jesus Christ. Only those who trust Christ's provision are God's children.

Here, each person must make a decision. Will you believe? Will you trust Christ's provision, accept His salvation, and be named as a child of God by faith? If you will, be sure that the blood of Jesus Christ will cleanse you from all your sins. (I John 1.7)

Satisfaction and Sufficiency

"The LORD is my shepherd; I shall not want. He maketh me to lie down in green pastures: he leadeth me beside the still waters." Psalm 23.1, 2

Some years ago my wife and I were acquainted with a woman, the mother of four boys. Her four boys had been fathered by three different men none of whom had been their mother's husband. Of those four boys, three of them found themselves in prison for lengthy sentences and only one made something good of himself.

After the third boy was sentenced to a long term in confinement, my wife and I went to visit the mother. The scene that lay before us was typical of the home – very untidy, with clothes, trash and dishes scattered all over so that finding a place to sit was a challenge.

She sat in her living room in tears and asked the question: "Why has God done this to me? I've been a good mother to my boys."

No one needs to stand in judgment in order to understand the problems that existed. No one needs to be a genius to understand that one cannot lead others in places where they have never been. In order for someone to be a good mother or a good father, that person first must be a good person. In order to lead in paths of righteousness, the leader must be righteous.

David exclaims, *"The LORD is my Shepherd."* Psalm 23 exposes Christ as the Great Shepherd who takes care of His sheep. He has led by example and has proven Himself to be someone worthy of being followed. When David says: "I shall not want," he indicates that every need shall be supplied in abundant fashion – God through Christ is sufficient to meet every need we have.

I am often amazed by the people Christians look to for counsel. The person at the local convenience store or the work-mate who has been married five or six times is not the one to whom we should turn when having marriage difficulties. The before mentioned woman would not be a good counselor when we are having difficulties with our children.

God's Word has the answer to every problem in life. Jesus is our Great Shepherd who has traveled every inch of life, experienced every good time and bad time, and has come through it victoriously. He is the one we should follow without question.

The result will be satisfaction because of the sufficiency of God's provision. We will lie down in green ("tender grass") pastures ("habitations"). Sheep lie down in green pastures only when they are filled completely – otherwise they are up eating. Only when they have eaten all they can hold and when they feel completely safe do they lie down to chew their cud.

The believer has this blessing from our Savior. Not only do we not lack for any good thing, we are safe and secure. We can be completely satisfied only when we allow our Savior to be the One doing the leading. Apart from Him, one's life can never be complete; but in Him, we can know complete fulfillment and total satisfaction.

When in difficulty, turn to Him. He will offer to you peace and contentment.

The King of Glory

"Lift up your heads, O ye gates; and be ye lift up, ye everlasting doors; and the King of glory shall come in. Who is this King of glory? The LORD strong and mighty, the LORD mighty in battle." Psalm 24.7, 8

That the world is filled with problems is no new news. It has always been that way. Problems are not new to God, just to us. We tend to examine and explain our personal history only by what we have experienced – never really considering how desperate times were in the past.

Today's Christians tend to believe themselves to be in the midst of perilous times – times when persecution has never been quite as it is today.

Of course, we must dismiss the Inquisition when believers were burned at the stake and other times in history when believers paid for their faith with their blood.

Our persecution comes more in the form of that uneasy feeling we get when we feel impressed to share our faith with the check-out clerk in the grocery store. After all, what will she think if I give her a Gospel tract or invite her to church? How will she respond to me the next time I must go to the store for groceries? She might think I'm weird.

It is believed that Psalm 24 was set during the time when the Ark of the Covenant was moved from the home of Obed Edom to Jerusalem. The Ark had been there for several years after it had been returned by the Philistines.

The Ark represented the presence and power of God in the midst of His people. Without the Ark, God seemed very far away. Any mention of God was made with baited breath – caution was the accepted practice. He seemed so impersonal – so distant.

At this point, David cries out with jubilation in respect of the return of the Ark – more importantly, of the return of the people to God.

Uncommon Praises from Common Psalms

"Lift up your heads!" "Look, He is here! God is where He has always been!"

It matters not what the persecution, or assumed persecution, when the believer senses the absence of God in his life, he wilts away in fear. The harshest persecutions are reserved for those who have the greatest faith. Only by having God very near can the believer conquer his personal fears.

What each of us needs to remember is that God is near – very near. He is with us no matter where we go or in what situation we may find ourselves. We need to lift up our heads from the worldly distractions. We need to move to a higher plane – the plane of spiritual awareness that God is present in our lives.

Victory over any problem or persecution is within reach; but it is only within reach if the King of Glory has come in. He is not far away – He desires fellowship with His children. If there has been a breach in your relationship with Him, go to Obed Edom's (where you left fellowship). He is still there – waiting for your return.

Remember that God has not left you – you have left Him. When you return, you will again bask in the glory of the Almighty – the One strong enough and powerful enough to cause you to praise Him in the middle of any persecution. Excitement will return to your life as you look unto Him. Salvation will again be fresh as you clean your hands and purify your heart. Fellowship will be sweet – as sweet as it was when you took your first step with Him.

Lift up your heads…and the King of Glory will come in!

Attitudes and Actions

"Shew me thy ways, O LORD; teach me thy paths." Psalm 25.4

When we were expecting our first baby, my wife and I became excited. Just think – a child – our child would soon be born.

Our church gave us a shower for the upcoming expectation. What a blessing! Among the items given were several cloth diapers. Today no one thinks of cloth diapers, but this was what seems to be many years ago.

As a new father, I took out one of the diapers, examined it, and began to install it. My mother-in-law stood quietly by watching as I tried to figure out what to do with the equipment. After having completed my new path, she gently stepped forward and said, "That looks good, but let me show you a better way."

My triumphant spirit was turned to something less than triumph – I was a bit crushed. I thought she would drool over my work and praise my effort. Not so. Although she had been kind and gentle, I rather resented her intrusion.

After getting over my pride, I realized that there was very little I could show or teach my mother-in-law about the care of babies. She had not only raised her own, but had successfully helped others in the care of their own children. She had learned the things that I needed to learn. She was the one who could teach me – if I had the proper attitude and actions. (I learned later how to properly use a cloth diaper. It is to be placed on one's shoulder for protection when burping a baby.)

In Psalm 25.4, David uses two different words, the meanings of which may be lost to the casual reader. The word "way" (derek) speaks of methods of operation including the attitudes behind those methods. The word "paths" (orach) speaks of direction of travel including the movement from one place to another.

Uncommon Praises from Common Psalms

The believer, although very active in the work, may lose the benefit of great reward due to an improper attitude. The attitude of our Lord was that he humbled himself in perfect submission to both the methods and attitudes of the Father. Not only did He do the work, but He also had the proper attitude toward the work. He was consistent in seeking the Father's will through prayer and obeyed with the right spirit.

The believer, then, must walk in the right paths – going down the road where the Savior leads. Our Savior's paths may not always prove to be the ones we would choose, but they are always best.

It may not make financial sense to give a tithe to the church. After all, we have needs of our own. It may not make social sense to attend church whenever the doors are open. After all, there is vacation, family, and activities.

To be right with God, however, means that His followers be followers both in attitude and action. God has been there since before we were created – the plan is His – the way is His – and our good takes priority in His thinking. Since He has our good in mind – bringing us to a place of spiritual maturity – the believer will never go wrong in walking in His path with a proper, submissive attitude.

Integrity

"Judge me, O LORD; for I have walked in mine integrity: I have trusted also in the LORD; therefore I shall not slide. Examine me, O LORD, and prove me; try my reins and my heart." Psalm 26:1, 2

Integrity is an easy concept to define but not so easy to maintain. The Old Testament uses the word to indicate someone who is "whole" or "complete." It parallels the New Testament word "perfect" – never suggesting sinless perfection but always someone who "has it together" spiritual.

The person who possesses integrity is one who is free from blemish. He need not shrink in fear when being questioned. He need not fear cross-examination. When confronted, the person who is lacking integrity often becomes argumentative and caustic. When he acts outside his established standard, he finds himself without foundation, becoming defensive when asked for reasons concerning his actions.

Paul says, *"All things are lawful unto me, but all things are not expedient..."* (1Cor. 6:12). Paul spoke of the liberty one has in his salvation as well as the believer's responsibility to act with expediency (with benefit and profit). Even though great authority and power may be granted to a leader, he must realize that when wielding that power he has a tremendous responsibility to do so with impunity – he must use that power and position for the benefit of those under him and for the good of the group.

Whenever any leader is suspected of abusing power or authority, his integrity is questioned and the respect others have for him is diminished. Those on the outside see hypocrisy, and those on the inside become frustrated. The organization he leads is in jeopardy.

Each of us should individually examine our lives thoroughly and often. It is enough to open God's Word and view its pages to see our own defects. The Word is the mirror through which we must make self-examination – through which we see our true self.

Uncommon Praises from Common Psalms

As we open God's Word, we should place ourselves alongside the Word in three areas. We should never compare ourselves with others – that would only skew the results of the tests.

We should ask God to examine us – that is, to scrutinize our lives and thoughts. Nothing should be reserved from His inspection. (Psalm 139.23, 24) He should have opportunity to prove us in order to determine our value and genuineness.

We should ask God to prove us – that is, to test our inner motivations. The word "prove" suggests a test by smelling. By smelling, one can determine whether something is fresh, stale, or rotten.

We should ask God to try us – that is, to work in us to make us better. The word "try" suggests the purification of precious metals. It is by the smelting process that the dross is removed so that the pure metal may be exhibited.

Being in a position of leadership offers the believer more privileges, but it also offers a greater responsibility to do the right thing. Believers should always strive toward maturity in Christ by allowing God, through His Word, to examine, prove, and try us. Believers should always guard their integrity for without it, they have no testimony worthy of emulation.

A One-Track Mind

"One thing have I desired of the LORD, that will I seek after; that I may dwell in the house of the LORD all the days of my life, to behold the beauty of the LORD, and to enquire in his temple." Psalm 27:4

I was recently reminded of a rather popular view of the differences between the way women and men think. At lunch a few days ago a young lady expressed it in terms that went something like this: men's minds are like waffles and women's minds are like spaghetti. Even though I didn't think either analogy was overly complimentary, she went on to make her case. It seems the waffle represents the man's compartmentalized thinking while the spaghetti represents the flowing together of all thoughts by women.

Men tend to think of one thing at a time while women think of many things all at once with all thoughts being connected. I will admit that it is sometimes frustrating to try to keep up in a conversation with my wife. From the perspective of my compartmentalization, she can shift gears, double clutch, and speed shift all at the same time. At times, she has shown great patience while I have tried to catch up – at other times, well, they were just other times.

All believers, whether with compartmentalized thinking or connective thinking, should have a one-track mind when it comes to spiritual things.

Whether the believer is experiencing good, or not so good, circumstances in life his heart should desire a closer walk with our Savior. Our Savior should be the first place we turn as we cast all our care on Him. Our eyes should be fastened on Him regardless of the situation or circumstances. The stare of the believer should always be in a heavenly direction towards our Advocate and Redeemer.

When money is tight, we should desire to sit with the Savior. When disaster strikes, there is no better place that at the Savior's side.

Uncommon Praises from Common Psalms

When all is well, the Savior's presence brings joy beyond human comprehension.

Only when the believer has a one-track mind, fastened and focused solely on the Lord Jesus Christ, will he find everlasting peace and satisfaction. Only then will the worries of this life fade into second hand concerns. Only then will the true believer understand the peace that passes all understanding.

Help

"Unto thee will I cry, O LORD my rock; be not silent to me: lest, if thou be silent to me, I become like them that go down into the pit." Psalm 28.1

I sat alone. Many had come by to offer their condolences. Many had prayed. Many revisited pains in their own lives as they had seen us, my family, suffering a great loss.

Now, the crowd was gone and I sat alone. No amount of conversation – no money – no great warm hugs would overcome that loneliness.

I trusted God completely (and still do), but in that hour trust gave way to tears. Tears that flowed freely between gasps for breath that wretched my chest nearly to convulsions. Alone, with nowhere and to no one with a salve that could ease the pain.

We have all at one time or another been faced with some type of an insurmountable problem – those circumstances in life when we have no answer to the looming problems we face. Money helps with the bills, but it does not solve heartaches. Hugs are warm and fuzzy, but they do not heal the broken. Visits from friends show that others care – but, ultimately, they sorrow with us and not for us.

When we face the unfathomable deep, the un-scalable height, the impassable expanse, there is only one way to turn – only One who can help. David said, *"Unto thee will I cry, O LORD my rock."* While the earth shakes and friends forsake, God is the immovable Rock – our Fortress – the One who not only sits us in our sorrow, but He also bears our sorrows for us.

David looks neither right nor left – he looks up. He fears neither circumstances nor abandonment. The only fear he faces is that God may turn a deaf ear (silent – "chashah" – "to be still, inactive, silent"). Should God abandon him, he would be no different than those with no hope. Should God be silent, he would be completely without a representative.

Uncommon Praises from Common Psalms

But God is never silent when His child needs solace. He may be speaking in a still, small voice. It is a voice so soft and tender that it may only be heard in a quiet place. Many times the voice is drowned by the din of crowds, mourners and comforters, who are trying to help.

In my darkest time, I was alone. That was the best place for me because my Rock had never moved. He was there – in the dark – through the sorrow – near enough for me to realize He cares.

The Voice

"The voice of the LORD..." Psalm 29

She was a small, petite, yet wiry lady. Born and raised in Idaho, she had become physically strong yet maintained a sweet spirit – at least most of the time. By most standards she had lived a hard life – working in the fields on her parents' farm – at times, harvesting corn and grain in the snow – feeding and milking cows before daylight in sub-zero weather.

She married my father at the age of 27. After coming to the Lord, Mom and Dad prayed for children – they had almost given up hope until their first child was born 12 years later – a direct answer to prayer. My older brother was born to her when she was 39 and I when she was 42. I was the child of her old age.

Even though she has been with the Lord for several years now, I remember her voice. Her voice was neither loud nor soft – just kind of normal. And, there were times I looked forward to hearing her voice – especially at supper time. Those were the times when she used her "Johnny" voice. But, there were other times – her "John Hundley Hill" voice. Same voice. Same person. Totally different situation.

The first time the word "voice" (Hebrew "qol") is used in the Scriptures is in Genesis 3.8. Up to this point, God had been walking with Adam and Eve in the Garden of Eden – in communion and fellowship – without encumbrances. After their disobedience, they hear His voice. Same voice. Same person. Totally different situation.

The times I was afraid to hear my mother's voice were when I was guilty. The times I was agitated or angered by her voice were those times when my argument had no basis. Most people become fearful when confronted with wrong and angered when their argument has no foundational truth. Being loud without foundation or forceful without consistency only serves to show great holes in a

Uncommon Praises from Common Psalms

person's character. ("Because I said so," and "Because I can," have never been good foundational points for arguments.)

"Qol" is a generic term referring to a person's voice – it can also refer to any sound. It could be the voice of a shepherd calling his sheep or the sound of a trumpet mustering troops for war. It could be the quiet cooing of a mother as she encourages her baby to sleep, or it could be the sound of the alarm startling the sleeper from his dreams.

God's voice is both gentle and forceful; it is both soothing and irritating. The application depends on your situation in life. When you are right with God, you long for the sound of His voice. When something stands between you and God, there is nothing He can say that will sound pleasing.

Psalm 29 shows God in His power – the sound of His voice causing all kinds of activity. He rides the flood and causes the thunder to roll. In His voice are storms that can tear up trees by their roots – He is the Mighty God.

That Mighty God is the same God who tenderly listens to His children. That Mighty God is the same God who holds us when we hurt and comforts us when we are lonely. That Voice – the voice that can create and destroy is the voice of the One who loves you and made open the Way of salvation.

If His voice angers or irritates, stop and discover the cause – it will be your situation in life. If His voice sooths and calms, thank God for His tender loving-kindness.

"Give unto the LORD the glory due unto his name; worship the LORD in the beauty of his holiness." (Psalm 29.2)

Night

"For his anger endureth but a moment; in his favour is life: weeping may endure for a night, but joy cometh in the morning." Psalm 30:5

A few years ago, our home was burglarized. Just a couple of months later, it happened again.

If you have ever had your home invaded, you will understand some of the angst (an unfounded feeling of anxiety) associated with the event. You feel violated and vulnerable. What had once been your private sanctuary had become somehow insecure. The locks had not stopped them – they took advantage and with it they took your "day-time living."

My wife no longer wanted to be at home; one of our daughters refused to be at home alone; and the other daughter – well, she put a softball bat beside her bed and hoped for an opportunity. As head of our home, I must admit there were several nights when I slept light – listening – waiting for a sound.

What was stolen in property compared little to what was taken emotionally. No matter where we were – no matter what time of day – for a long while it was night.

We invested in a home security system – alarm and video. We reinforced the locks and doors. After all that, I had to come to the realization that if someone wants in badly enough, they will get in. The perpetrators of the crime are in prison – but they will not be there forever. And, even if they never come back, there are others who could be just as accommodating.

During his first inaugural address, President Roosevelt said, "Only Thing We Have to Fear Is Fear Itself" (FDR's First Inaugural Address). In some ways he was correct; fear is a matter of a wrong focus. The believer's focus should not be centered around alleviating fear, but in focusing on the Light. Even though the night is long and dark, it must eventually give way to day. We weep and mourn during the night of gloom and despair because of the fear it brings. The day brings new light – a new opportunity – a clear view of things as they really are.

It matters not what puts you into a night season, the answer is always the same – Jesus. He is the Bright and Morning Star – the light of the world. We weep and fear because we have no clear view of God in His majesty. Abundant living can come only as we see things from a heavenly view – a view that is lighted by God Himself.

People, events, and circumstances can plague us only so long as we maintain an earthly view of living – so long as we hold to earthly possessions and long for earthly approval. Biblically, it is only God whom we need to please. "In His favor is living" – life abundant and eternal. Night turns to day.

www.ingramcontent.com/pod-product-compliance
Lightning Source LLC
Chambersburg PA
CBHW061511040426
42450CB00008B/1563